An Unofficial Joke Book for Fans of ROBLOX

An Unofficial Joke Book for Fans of ROBLOX

800 HILARIOUSLY BLOCKHEADED JOKES TO LEVEL UP YOUR LAUGHTER

Brian Boone
Illustrated by Amanda Brack

Sky Pony Press
New York

An Unofficial Joke Book for Fans of Roblox. Copyright © 2022 by Hollan Publishing, Inc.

Sky Pony Press books may be purchased in bulk at special discounts for sales promotion, corporate gifts, fund-raising, or educational purposes. Special editions can also be created to specifications. For details, contact the Special Sales Department, Sky Pony Press, 307 West 36th Street, 11th Floor, New York, NY 10018 or info@skyhorsepublishing.com.

Sky Pony® is a registered trademark of Skyhorse Publishing, Inc.®, a Delaware corporation.

Visit our website at www.skyponypress.com.

10 9 8 7 6 5 4 3 2

Library of Congress Cataloging-in-Publication Data is available on file.

Cover design by Brian Peterson
Cover illustration by Amanda Brack

Hardcover ISBN: 978-1-5107-7530-5
E-book ISBN: 978-1-5107-7604-3

Printed in the United States of America

CONTENTS

Introduction

Welcome Roblox players and curious Robloxians!
As a frequenter of Roblox's numerous enchanting experiences, you know that Roblox isn't a video game—it's a way of life! It's a platform where millions of avid programmers and excited players can make, share, and play video games.

And there are *thousands* of them, designed by people from all around the world that provide endless hours of entertainment in the form of adventure games, games that simulate real world experiences, games that bring fantasy realms to life, and games that are just plain full of fun.

You know what else is fun to make, share, and play around with? Jokes! We combined these two fantastic pastimes into *An Unofficial Joke Book for Fans of Roblox*. From noobs to pros, this book mines explosive enjoyment (and a lot of silliness, goofiness, laughs, and chuckles) out of some of the most popular Roblox games and areas out there, including Adopt Me, Build a Boat for Treasure, Jailbreak, Work at a Pizza Place, and a whole lot more.

We hope you'll get your Robux's worth!

Chapter 1
ALL ABOUT ROBLOX

Let's dive in and have a few laughs with these completely ridiculous jokes about Roblox itself—the community, the culture, and the day-to-day life of being a Roblox player.

What's the highest point in Roblox?
Up on the r-OOF.

•

Why couldn't the Roblox player build anything shiny?
They lost their marbles.

•

Why did the Roblox game disappear right after the player made it?
It wasn't up to code.

•

Where's a good place to invest your Robux?
In the block market.

Why did Officer Zombie
fall asleep?

Because he was dead tired.

Did you hear about the Roblox player with a cold?
Her nose was totally bloxed.

Why can't you score against Roblox players at basketball?
All of the blox.

●

Knock-knock!
Who's there?
Reee!
Whoa, calm down and I'll let you in.

●

Knock-knock!
Who's there?
Mike.
Mike who?
Mike up!

●

Knock-knock!
Who's there?
Icc.
Ice who?
Ice to sec you!

Knock-knock!
Who's there?
Wood.
Wood who?
Wood you please open the door?

•

Knock-knock!
Who's there?
Planks.
Planks who?
You're welcome.

•

What Roblox building material smells like fish?
Plank-ton.

•

How do you play a joke on someone in Roblox?
You pull a plank!

Why didn't the Roblox player build any buildings today?
She wasn't slated to.

What kind of party do
Roblox players like best?

A lua -au!

Why did the Roblox player want to grow up to be a heart surgeon?

Because she heard she'd learn how to bypass!

•

How do Roblox characters bake bread?

They start with Jane Dough.

•

What's the most powerful club in Roblox?

The Builders Club.

•

Why can't so many Roblox characters defend themselves?

Because they're unarmed.

•

Look close in Roblox and you'll find James Bond.

He's agent 00F.

•

Why should you give your Roblox character a hand?

Because it probably wasn't built with any.

What do you call someone who gets banned from Roblox?
Blocked.

●

I was so upset when my player got killed in Roblox.
I fell to pieces!

●

I'm not sure why I like Roblox so much.
I guess it just puts a smile on my face.

●

What do "ABC" and a busy Roblox player have in common?
Neither stands for anything!

●

Ever play around on that Roblox world made completely out of concrete?
It's hard!

What kind of music do Roblox players like best?
RAP music.

Why do actors like to mess around in Roblox?
Because there's always a script.

Why is Roblox so cool?
Because there's always an A/C.

What's a Roblox player's least favorite subject in school?
Band.

What's a Roblox builder's favorite dessert?
Cobbler.

I understand why you built a whole game out of glass.
It's so transparent!

What do dogs in Roblox say?

"W-OOF!"

Where should you never play Roblox?

In a beaned-bag chair.

Roblox Player #1: Why do you like making new games?
Roblox Player #2: I don't know, I guess I'm just
ac-custom-ed to it.

•

Those who live in glass houses probably wouldn't like my
new Roblox game, "Let's Throw Stones at Glass Houses."

•

When is a field not a field but also a field?
When it's a forcefield.

•

What fruit grows wild in Roblox?
Pome-granites.

•

What's the worst OS for playing Roblox?
AOS!

•

What do Boosted Apes drink?
Boosted Ape juice.

What insult do Roblox players take as a compliment?
Blockhead!

•

How many bricks does it take to finish a Roblox tower made entirely of bricks?
One, as it's the last one that finishes the tower.

•

How do you keep your Roblox pajamas from escaping?
Robe locks!

•

What's a salmon's favorite game?
Roe-blox!

•

Did you hear about the Roblox movie?
It's going to be a bloxbuster!

You're a really great Roblox player.

But don't get a big head about it or anything.

Why don't NPCs get invited to parties?
Because they're so square.

Why didn't the souped-up bed do much damage in BedWars?

It was two-tired.

How can you stop from getting beaned?

Try Bean-O!

Knock-knock!
Who's there?
Lua.
Lua who?
Lua me? Lua you?

Knock-knock!
Who's there?
Obby.
Obby who?
Obby out here until you let me in.

Knock-knock!
Who's there?
Oof.
Oof who?
Oof are *you*?

Knock-knock!
Who's there?
BB.
BB who?
Waaaaaah!

Knock-knock!
Who's there?
EZ.
EZ who?
EZ does it!

What did the banned Roblox
player eat for dinner?

Beans!

Knock-knock!

Who's therc?

LMaD.

LMaD who?

LMaDies and gentlemen, Roblox!

Knock-knock!
Who's there?
IC.
IC who?
IC what you did there.

Knock-knock!
Who's there?
IC.
IC who?
IC out here, I'm cold, so let me in!

Knock-knock!
Who's there?
PS.
PS who?
PS I love you!

Knock-knock!
Who's there?
Bean.
Bean who?
Bean kicked off Roblox!

Knock-knock!
Who's there?
Skid.
Skid who?
Let's you and me skidoo on out of here!

What's a Robloxer's favorite candy?
Reeeee's Pieces

Is Roblox hard?
No, it's as easy as learning your ABCs.

You can't just play Roblox, you have to make something
original.
It's the custom!

●

Why is every day spent in Roblox a good day?
Because every day in Roblox is an appy day!

●

Knock-knock!
Who's there?
Dave the Animal.
Dave the Animal who?
Wait, no, I want to be Cool Kevin.
That will cost you 1,000 Robux.

●

I just spent a lot of Robux changing my ID, but it's okay, my
new one is awesome.
It's a real name-changer.

Do Roblox characters use
the bathroom?

Yes, they go to the John Doe.

Why should you bring a bottle of glue to Roblox?
Because of all the models.

Knock-knock!

Who's there?

Dyna.

Dyna who?

DynaBlast in there and play with you!

•

Why do photographers like Roblox?

Because of all the models.

•

Knock-knock!

Who's there?

Arrow.

Arrow who?

Arrow on the side of caution and be careful in that obby!

•

Knock-knock

Who's there?

Amaze.

Amaze who?

A maze will end if you follow the arrows on the ground.

Knock-knock!
Who's there?
Quest.
Quest who?
It's me!

How does a Robloxer laugh?
Bruh-huh-huh.

Did you hear about the big Roblox fight?
Talk about a bruh-ha-ha.

Parent: Did you give the dog water?
Roblox Kid: No way, he's a great Roblox player!

How do Robloxers start their day?
With a hot cup of KO-KO.

What happened when the Roblox builder didn't use enough supports?

She was on the brick of disaster.

What pets do Robloxers have?

Cat-alogs.

What do Robloxers look for in the woods?
Cata-logs.

●

Roblox Proverb: If you can make it here you can make it anywhere . . . else on Roblox.

●

Roblox Proverb: If you dream it you can make it . . . if you know basic programming.

●

Roblox Proverb: It's all about three things in here: stats, cats, and hats.

●

What's another name for a wild game hunt?
Roblox!

●

What's the best way to get into Roblox?
Just get with the program!

I can't play Roblox because I don't have a PC, only a video
game system.

Hey, console yourself!

•

Being a young Roblox designer is a lot like trying to drive a car.
It's hard to see past the dashboard.

•

What do you call a messed-up Roblox server?

A swerver.

•

How is Roblox like a baby?

It goes through a lot of changes every day.

•

**What sounds like a rodent but is something you want a
lot of?**

Badges!

Having a lot of Robux . . .
It just makes cents!

•

What kind of guy works in a Roblox Studio?
A dude-io!

•

What should you wear to a fancy Roblox party?
A tie-coon.

•

What sports team would cost the most in Robloxia?
The Milwaukee Robux.

•

Roblox isn't all that expensive.
And after you buy it, you can get a robate.

•

What's a good name for an expert at obstacle courses?
Bobby!

How are obstacle courses made?
It's somebody's jobby to make a nice obby!

●

When you buy Roblox at a store, how does it come?
In a Robox!

●

What's the best way through an obstacle course?
While riding an obstacle horse!

●

What do you call someone who gets upset when they get beaned?
A beanie baby!

●

Knock-knock!
Who's there?
Badge.
Badge who?
Stop badgering me!

How is going away on vacation and leaving Roblox at home like a Muppet?
Because you miss Piggy.

●

Knock-knock!
Who's there?
Bed.
Bed who?
Bed hair day!

●

Roblox Player #1: You look like you've got bed hair.
Roblox Player #2: Hey, this cost me a lot of Robux!

●

You Know You Play Too Much Roblox If . . .
■ You refuse to eat beans.

■ Someone asks you to unplug a cord so you cancel your Discord account.

- You eat all your meals off of diamond plates.

- You call actual babies Newbs.

- You take Pal Hair with your eggs.

- You get such good grades you expect to see diamonds on your report card.

- You draw all your Os sideways and crooked.

- You see a sign that says "merge," you think it's heading to the Neon Cave.

- When you're lonely, you look all around for an E button.

- You don't sleep, you "Zzzz."

- You don't take "fat legs" as an insult.

- You don't call it art class, you call it Free Paint.

- You call your sibling your bruh-ther.

- At restaurants, you ask the server to load a game.

You Know You Play Too Much Roblox When...

You'll eat your vegetables, but only if you can put them on your head and call them salad hair.

■ You tried to get sent home from school with a case of Football Fever.

- You write TY notes.

- You don't stay "OW" when you get hurt, you say "WO."

- You want to be a bricklayer when you grow up.

- You always look for the arrows on the ground, to find a proper exit.

Chapter 2
SPHERE IT IS!

What do you get when you cross a cute town, cute circular animals, and an obsession with fishing? The delightful Roblox game MeepCity—which is also home to a lot of jokes and humor.

What do you call an obstacle course in MeepCity?
A blobby obby!

●

How'd they create such a unique surface in the Plaza?
Actually, they just cobbled it together.

●

Why did the player build a Wizard Tower?
He needed to take a wizard.

●

How do you build a Wizard Tower?
Magic!

How many fish can you
put in an empty bucket?

One. After that it isn't
empty anymore.

Knock-knock!

Who's there?

Me.

Me who?

Wow, a talking cat!

Knock-knock!
Who's there?
Map.
Map who?
Map who smells awful, I should flush!

●

What part of MeepCity smells the worst?
Big Gassy.

●

How to describe the fisherman in MeepCity?
He looks like a plaid dad, and that's totally rad.

●

Have you seen the fisherman's outfit?
Yeah, he's the vest!

●

The fish in MeepCity don't have eyes.
So technically they're FSH.

Robloxer #1: Do you like fishing in MeepCity?
Robloxer #2: I'm hooked!

What's the MeepCity fisherman's name?
Rod!

Robloxer #1: Want to go fishing?
Robloxer #2: No, that's not something I want to tackle.

Why and how did everyone in MeepCity agree to fish?
They took a pole!

What's the most popular card game in MeepCity?
Go Fish.

Are Meeps cute?
Yes, the eyes have it!

Robloxer #1: I see snowballs are around in MeepCity.
Robloxer #2: Yeah, snowballs are like that everywhere!

●

Knock-knock!
Who's there?
Snowball.
Snowball who?
Snowball could be found so the Starball game was cancelled.

●

I was overwhelmed by the number of snowballs I just saw in
    MeepCity.
It was just a lot to pack in.

●

Knock-knock!
Who's there?
Icy.
Icy who?
Icy a lot of snowy snowballs in Mcep City!

I love playing Starball.
You could say it's my number one obby.

•

Which Meeps smell the worst?
Oders.

•

What fish used to smell but don't anymore?
Smelt!

•

Knock-knock!
Who's there?
So selfish!
So selfish who?
So selfish if you want to make it in MeepCity.

•

Can you take care of bodily functions in MeepCity?
Sure, there are piers all over the place.

How is fishing in MeepCity like a movie?
A big cast.

•

**What's the difference between real life fishing and
MeepCity fishing?**
One is about bites and the other is about bytes.

•

What kind of fish are worth the most?
Goldfish!

•

Which MeepCity fish is the fastest?
The ones that get away!

•

**It's such a nice setup they've got in MeepCity for people
to get food and income sources.**
It's very so-fish-ticated.

•

I caught five fish in a minute.
It was a very ef-fish-ent use of my time.

How do you communicate
with the fish?

Just drop them a line.

What did the rod say to the fish?

"Catch you later!"

Knock-knock!
Who's there?
Fish.
Fish who?
Fish you so much, buddy, let's hang out more often.

Knock-knock!
Who's there?
Lake.
Lake who?
Lake to go fishing with me?

Getting all the fish I'm able to is something I've always
    wanted to do in MeepCity.
It's on my bucket list!

Knock-knock!
Who's there?
Philip.
Philip who?
Philip a bucket with fish!

What can you add to a bucket that will make all the fish inside disappear?

A hole.

●

All the fish in MeepCity are so colorful. So what kind of fish are they?

Rainbow trout!

●

Knock-knock!

Who's there?

Halo!

Halo who?

Halo to you, too!

●

Knock-knock!

Who's there?

Cloak.

Cloak who?

Cloak who?! You call me crazy?

If you want to buy a toy for
your Meep, get a unicycle.

It's wheely fun!

Which hat is made of pizza?

The Domino crown.

What?

Oh, sorry I couldn't hear you.

I didn't have my dog ears on.

●

I was going to buy some dog ears.

But the price was ruff.

●

Roblox Player #1: Why are you crying? We're just playing MeepCity!

Roblox Player #2: I'm sorry, it's just so full of emotions!

●

What's in the middle of MeepCity that's *not* in the middle of MeepCity?

A big space!

●

What's the last thing you should buy at the Furniture Store?

An End Table!

When is being in the pits
a good thing?

When you're in the Ball Pit
you bought at the Furniture
Store in MeepCity!

I can really see myself in one of these mirrors from the
Furniture Store.

When is being dead a good thing in MeepCity?
When you're using an emotion.

•

I used a MeepCity emote at the gas station.
I guess I was just pumped!

•

I wanted to dress my Meep up like a chicken
But it cried fowl.

•

Why is the Meep alphabet so different from English?
There are two big I's in the middle.

•

Knock-knock!
Who's there?
Hats.
Hats who?
Oh, you must be playing MeepCity.

44

Roblox Player #1: Do you like MeepCity?
Roblox Player #2: I'm having a ball!

What's a better name for the Pet Shop?
The small ball mall!

What's another name for MeepCity?
Adopt Meep!

The winner of Daytona 500 gets $2 million, which is 160
million Robux. Think of how much MeepCity racing
that driver would have to do to get all that!

How can you block ropes?
With a rope blocker.

We bought some decorations at the Furniture Store.
It was a banner day!

What can you write on
with a Big Pencil?

A big notepad!

**What did the Big Bad Wolf say when he played
MeepCity?**

"My, what big eyes they have!"

What's the least smart way to use your money at the Furniture Store?
Dumbbells!

•

Roblox Player #1: Years later I still regret not buying that mannequin.
Roblox Player #2: Still?

•

I'm enjoying my new bubble machine.
It really pops!

•

Knock-knock!
Who's there?
Chair.
Chair who?
Chair's the furniture I just bought!

•

What's the most dangerous place in a MeepCity home?
The Bean Bag!

You know you play a lot of MeepCity if . . .

You draw every E with
a little top hat.

- When your teacher asks you to name all the states, you reply, "Small, Medium, Rock, Trailer, Igloo . . . "

- You tried to do some home improvements by throwing some coins at your house.

- You went fishing, caught a bunch, and were disappointed you didn't haul in any money.

- You call a football field "Big Grassy."

- You think the best way to go fishing is to look for the dark spots.

- After a big accomplishment, you celebrate by sleeping.

- You never hesitate to clap for yourself.

- You wonder why real traffic cones don't sparkle.

Chapter 3
GET A PET AND YOU'RE SET!

Adopt Me is one of the most popular (and enjoyable games) on all of Roblox. It's a wide, wild world of creatures and critters, and these jokes celebrate them all.

Roblox Player #1: How are the game mechanics in Adopt Me?
Roblox Player #2: Egg-cellent!

•

How does a Robloxer describe a rainstorm?
"It's hatching like cats and dogs out there!"

•

What instrument does a unicorn play?
Something in the horn section.

•

Did you hear about the guy who spent all his time finding dragon eggs in Adopt Me?
He was fired!

Roblox Player #1: How's your
history in finding Safari Eggs?

Roblox Player #2: Spotty!

LOADING....

I just love those Diamond Egg pets.
I really took a shine to them.

51

What's a recently hatched llama's favorite game?
Robllox.

Knock-knock!
Who's there?
Owl?
Owl who?
Exactly.

Where might you find an Aussie Egg?
Down under.

What just-hatched animal is still covered in shell?
A turtle!

How can you tell if an Aussie Egg will give you a kangaroo?
It jumps!

Knock-knock!
Who's there?
Mythic.
Mythic who?
I mythic you, too.

●

Where can you still find a Mythic Egg?
Phoenix!

●

Roblox Player #1: How'd your meeting with Doug go?
Roblox Player #2: It was ruff.

●

How is Doug like a tree?
All that bark.

●

What kind of NPC is Holly?
A purrrrrfect one.

Why is Speedy the Penguin so likable?
Oh, he's just an ice guy!

**

I just went to the Neon Cave.
I give it a glowing review!

**

Why is the Ruler's Castle so great?
Because it rules!

**

Where might you find a yard stick?
In the Ruler's Castle.

**

What place in Adopt Me is made out of itself?
The Treehouse.

**

What kind of meat is popular in Adopt Me?
Pork shops!

Roblox Player #1: I bought you
a Gingerbread house.

Roblox Player #2: How sweet!

Roblox Player #1: Do you like Lunar House?

Roblox Player #2: I'm over the moon!

Did you visit the hospital in Adopt Me?
It's totally sick!

●

I'm going to buy the Futuristic House.
When? Tomorrow.

●

Roblox Player #1: How's the Fairy House?
Roblox Player #2: Not good or bad.

●

Where can you *not* find a baby in Adopt Me?
At the Baby Shop.

●

Knock-knock!
Who's there?
Horse Cycle.
Horse Cycle who?
Horse Cycle your garbage!

Knock-knock!
Who's there?
Baby Shop.
Baby Shop who?
Baby shop, do do do do do do, Baby Shop . . .

●

How is Adopt Me like raising real kids?
The kids disappeared!

●

How are Adopt Me and this book different?
The eggs have yolks, and the book has jokes.

●

Why is Adopt Me the best game to play before breakfast?
All the eggs!

●

I couldn't figure out how to get any more animals in Adopt
    Me.
And then I cracked it!

What are the odds of a Safari Egg hatching into a giraffe?

Tall!

Why did the chicken cross the road?

It was after a rare Fossil Egg it dropped.

Is Adopt Me healthy?

Sure, it provides a lot of eggs-cerise.

Are the animals free in Adopt Me?
No, they cost eggs-tra.

●

Can you cut open an egg in Adopt Me?
No, you hatchet.

●

Parent: Why didn't you go to sleep?
Kid: I was up all night tending to my unborn animals.
Parent: That's no eggs-cuse!

●

Can you steal eggs in Adopt Me?
No, but you can poach them!

●

Who's the most popular singer in Adopt Me?
Drake.

●

Roblox Player #1: I bought a great new potion in Adopt Me.
Roblox Player #2: Fine, but don't get a Big Head about it.

Knock-knock!
Who's there?
Grow.
Grow who?
Grow away!

Knock-knock!
Who's there?
Big Head.
Big Head who?
Big Head on in there if you'll let me in.

Knock-knock!
Who's there?
Shell.
Shell who?
Shell your promo codes with me!

What's the best way to find new creatures in Adopt Me?

Go eggs-ploring.

Knock-knock!

Who's there?

Shell.

Shell who?

Shell you buy something with your Robux?

Knock-knock!

Who's there?

Horse Cycle.

Horse Cycle who?

Horse Cycles are forming it's so cold out here!

Knock-knock!

Who's there?

Dragon.

Dragon who?

These jokes just dragon and on.

Knock-knock!

Who's there?

Aurora.

Aurora who?

Aurora going to open the door or not?

Knock-knock!
Who's there?
Seal.
Seal who?
My lips are sealed until you let me in.

Why does Eggburt wear glasses?
They make his vision eggs-cellent.

Knock-knock!
Who's there?
Henry.
Henry who?
Henry body gonna let me in?

Why is Speedy always ready?
Because he's always on board!

How did the game designer keep the Snowy Shop standing?
Iglooed it!

•

What does an Adopt Me player say when their game doesn't go their way?
OOFington!

•

In what case should you always bring your own bags to the Green Groceries?
Justin case!

•

What's the difference between a rare insect pet and the head of Adopt Me?
One is a *lady*bug and one is a *Sir* Woofington.

•

What three composers do those chickens like best?
Bach, Bach, Bach!

Where did the pig go when it died?
Hog Heaven.

What do you call and Adopt Mc pig with three eyes?
A piiig!

What would you get if you put a saddle on a pig?
A road hog.

Where do Adopt Me pigs sleep?
In ham-mocks.

Did you hear about newly hatched showoff pig?
What a ham!

What are the most musical pets in Adopt Me?
The bandicoot!

What happens when an Adopt Me cow wanders into a computer running Roblox?

It turns into an e-mu.

●

What animal is still alive when it croaks?

A frog!

●

What cracks fast but moves slow?

A turtle.

●

What animal can sing, dance, and act?

The hawk—it has many talons!

●

What band do scarabs like best?

The Beetles!

●

What animal might you find in a church?

A St. Bernard.

Knock-knock!
Who's there?
Fairy.
Fairy who?
Fairy pleased to see you!

What animals live deep below the surface?
Abyss-inian cats.

•

Where can you find the Roblox TV show?
On Peacock!

•

I was going to try to find a sloth.
But I was too lazy to look for one.

•

Knock-knock.
Who's there?
Bee.
Bee who?
Bee opening the door for me now?

•

What do ice golems love to eat?
Ice scream!

How do ice golems travel?
They ride their icicles.

Knock-knock!
Who's there?
Adopt Me.
Adopt who?
Adopt Me pencil on the ground and it rolled away.

Knock-knock!
Who's there?
Hatch.
Hatch who?
Bless you!

What's an ice golem's favorite game?
Freeze tag.

Where do you take a sick horse in Adopt Me?
To the horse-pital!

What kind of flowers do sick unicorns like best?
Horse-petals.

You know you play a lot of Adopt Me if . . .

■ When you open a carton of eggs, you wait for them to hatch into pets.

■ When you open a carton of eggs, you're disappointed they don't have little hats or crowns on.

■ You don't think eggs are expired, only "limited edition" ones.

Chapter 4

IT'S A CHEESY JOB, BUT SOMEBODY'S GOT TO DO IT

Have you ever wanted to work at a pizza place? Well then, you've probably gotten a taste of that with Roblox's well-played Work at a Pizza Place simulation game. Now have a hot, sizzling slice of jokes about it!

Why do they write orders in black ink on a white board at Builder Brothers?
Because if they used a blackboard nobody would be able to see them.

•

Work at a Pizza Place is my favorite Roblox game.
I never sausage a fun place!

•

What happened when the pizza cook left the sauce out?
The sauce aged and turned into sausage.

Customer: How's the sausage
 here at Builder Brothers?

Cashier: It's the wurst!

What kind of sausage can you even find online?
Links!

Where did Builder Brothers get its sausage, pepperoni, and cheese pizza recipe?

Grease!

Can you get bacon on your pizza?

Sure, if your hair falls on it.

What do you call someone who makes the perfect sausage pizza?

A big wiener!

What kind of music plays during sausage pizza making?

Nothing but bangers!

The sausages got stuck in the oven, so the cook pulled and pulled and now it's pulled pork.

A pizza walked into Builders Brothers and ordered a pizza. They gave it to him because they served food there.

●

Cook #1: Can you make me a pizza with this little sausage?
Cook #2: Sure, it won't be long.

●

Knock-knock!
Who's there?
Salami.
Salami who?
Salami a sausage pizza, please.

●

The silly cashier asked what kind of pizza to make and the customer said "cheese," and so the cashier took her picture.

●

How do you repair a broken pizza?
With tomato paste.

Knock-knock!
Who's there?
Puppy.
Puppy who?
Puppy-roni pizza please!

The cook put all the pizza place's sausage and pepperoni on
    one pizza and now they're totally out.
Top that!

What's the most crucial part of a pizza joke?
The delivery.

Roblox Player #1: Want to hear a joke about a pizza place?
Roblox Player #2: Not if it's too cheesy.

What tastes like pizza and is invisible?
Invisible pizza.

Customer: How do I know you'll make the pizza right?
Cashier: Crust us!

•

There's another pizza place in Roblox that only serves crab
    and lobster pizza.
It's called the Crust Station.

•

Why doesn't Builder Brothers give away their pizza?
Because then they'd be out of dough.

•

Builder Brothers was going to start making frozen pizza.
But the idea wasn't very thawed out.

•

Why is making a pizza easy?
Because cheesy does it!

•

What's the best way to burn thousands of calories quickly?
Leave a pizza in the oven.

How do they keep the sausage
healthy at the pizza place?

They take it for a walk in the pork.

The cook cut 300 pizzas in an hour.
He was rolling along!

Did you hear about the fancy digital pizza slicers?
It's cutting-edge tech!

Knock-knock!
Who's there?
Pizza.
Pizza who?
Pizza cheese and two pieces of pepperoni please!

Customer: I ordered a pizza with yellow cheese, sausage, and pepperoni?
Cashier: How was it?
Customer: Eh, meaty-ochre.

What is Work at a Pizza Place but an experience for which you don't need any previous experience to experience!

Why do hippies visit the pizza parlor?

They just want piece, man.

When does a pizza cost the least Robux?

When you have a coupon.

Why did the pizza want to get out of the store?
It felt boxed in.

How do you make a soda pop?
Put a Fizzly in the oven.

I couldn't tell if it was a Double Value order
And then it came to me . . . in a flash!

What is cold but burns?
A can of Fizzly.

Knock-knock!
Who's there?
Mustache.
Mustache who?
Mustache you what kind of pizza you want to order!

Knock-knock!
Who's there?
Pizza.
Pizza who?
I'm going to give you a pizza my mind!

●

Knock-knock!
Who's there?
Brothers.
Brothers who?
Brothers who make pizza!

●

Knock-knock!
You don't have to knock, we're a business. Come on in!

●

What can't you park outside Builder Brothers Pizza?
Three cars.

●

What are the Builder Brothers' first names?
I have no idea, but they sure do make a good pizza.

Cashier: This pizza is covered in insects.

Cook: Hey, don't let it bug you.

Why were the employees hitting each other?
Because they were in the boxing room.

Why were the cook's pants covered in pizza?
Because he put on the conveyor belt.

•

When do the most pizza orders come through?
On Boxing Day.

•

What's that area right by the pizza place called?
Who cares, it's a real dump.

•

What else does Cook make?
Cookies!

•

Why didn't the delivery car move?
It was on brake.

•

Can a chicken work at the pizza place?
Yes, it can bok-bok-box.

What pizza ingredient might you find walking around the forest?
The dough!

•

A customer came into Builder Brothers and asked for a
popperoni pizza.
So the cook spilled a Fizzly on it.

•

Where's the secret spot in Work at a Pizza Place?
Well, it's a secret!

•

Customer: Can I get eggs on my pizza?
Cashier: Only if you order it eggs-press!

•

Who were the Builder Brothers parents?
Mr. and Mrs. Builder Brother.

•

Customer: No mozzarella sticks on the menu?
Cashier: No, mozzarella sticks to the pizza.

What do you call the bugs on a dropped pizza?
Moth-arellas.

Why did the happy customer leave Builder Brothers?
Because she was fed up.

Customer: This is a whole block of cheese on here.
Cook: Yeah, it's not so grate.

The pizza wanted to be in a school play, but it never happened.
It was always getting cut.

Customer #1: This pizza is covered in tiny bugs, but I think
I'm going to eat it anyway.
Customer #2: Weird flecks, but okay.

When's the best time to hit Builder Brothers?
On Pie-Day!

When's the best time to hit Builder Brothers?
About pie o'clock.

•

Customer #1: Hey look at all those people back there making pizzas!
Customer #2: What a cheesy line!

•

"I hate thick bread under cheese and pepperoni," the Robloxer said, crustily.
"Where's the cheese?" asked the Robloxer gratingly.

•

Roblox Player #1: That pizza maker put double cheese on my pizza!
Roblox Player #2: How dairy!

•

How do you make a pepperoni pizza?
With lots of pepperation.

Does cheese have muscles?

Yeah, it's totally shredded!

What kind of pizza flies right out of the pizza parlor?
Plain.

Why did the customer order a pizza with just a little bit of tomatoes?

Because they were a little saucy.

●

What kind of tomato smells the best?

A roma.

●

Roblox Player #1: We never did order a pizza.

Roblox Player #2: How come?

Roblox Player #1: We couldn't decide what kind to get. We just went around in circles.

●

Ordering a pizza is always a popular decision.
It's an idea that can be roundly agreed on!

●

Why'd they change the name to Builder Brothers Pizza from Hot and Fresh Pizza?

Because the pizza got cold and old.

You know you play at a lot of Work at a Pizza Place if . . .

- When you find a locked door, you figure that's where a manager is hiding.

- At a store and you want to speak to the manager, you look for the "remove manager" button instead.

- You go on a break and expect to instantly head home and for your clothes to change.

- You put down your experience playing the game on your resume.

Chapter 5

FUN DOESN'T GROW ON TREES, IT GROWS UNDER THEM

You're really going to "dig" this part of the book . . . because it's all about the dangerously delicious Roblox land of Blox Fruits.

How come the fruits in Blox Fruits don't rot in the sun?

They're covered in sunblox!

•

There are so many different, specific Blox Fruits.

But the devil is in the details!

•

Why are Blox Fruits also called Devil Fruits?

Because the game is so hot!

What's the difference between real-life fruit and Blox Fruit?
Real fruit keeps you alive, while Blox Fruit can kill.

•

What kind of parties do they have in Blox Fruits?
Block parties.

•

No matter how much Robux you spend on fruit . . .
It's always going to be a square meal.

•

Want to hear a joke about spawning?
Sorry, you waited too long. Come back in an hour.

•

What's another name for Blox Fruits buying and selling?
The Block Market.

•

What do you call a bunch of burned fruit?
Cinder Blox.

What fruit will always hide
in your shoes for months?

Sand!

Do surfers like Blox Fruits?

Yeah, they think it's totally cubular!

Robloxer #1: Do you like Blox Fruits?
Robloxer #2: It rings my beli!

●

What does a Robloxer wear on their pants?
A beli.

●

How are super-fast Blox Fruits like real fruits?
They can make you run fast, just like sugar!

●

Which kind of Fruit would you find in the middle of the alphabet?
LMN-tal.

●

Does the Castle on the Sea raid have an official rating?
Yes, it's rated argh!

●

Did you know? You can buy corn fruit from a pirate.
It costs a buccaneer.

Unfortunately, you can't play the pirate portions of Blox Fruits today.
You'll need a patch.

●

Robloxer #1: Why shouldn't I fall into a water during a raid?
[Falls, incurs damage]
Robloxer #2: Sea!

●

Basic Sword: Hey I'm a good weapon.
Me: You have a good point.

●

Robloxer #1: Do you like my new sword?
Robloxer #2: Sure, it's looking sharp!

●

Somebody stole my own sword and beaned me with it.
What a cutthroat game!

In Blox Fruits, you have to work your way up to the best
    swords.

Some are a cut above the rest.

●

Knock-knock!

Who's there?

Sword.

Sword who?

Sword your weapons, they're too many and they're
    disorganized!

●

Knock-knock!

Who's there?

Sword.

Sword who?

Sword of a stupid question, yeah?

●

"Watch what my sword can do!" the Robloxer said cuttingly.

Knock-knock!
Who's there?
Gun.
Gun who?
Gun come in there soon.

●

What other game do Blox Fruit players also like to play?
Cross sword puzzles.

●

What's a good fruit for discarding weapons you don't need?
The litter blox.

●

Knock-knock!
Who's there?
May.
May who?
May lay going on out here!

Knock-knock!
Who's there?
Melee.
Melee who?
Melee down a minute; I'm tired from all the fighting.

•

I only use a sword every seven days.
On a weakly basis.

•

What fruit only grows in March, April, and May?
Spring!

•

What fruit will just jump right out at you?
Spring!

•

Is there a store for fruit?
Sure, the Chop Shop.

What happens to the pig who
fell in the ground in Blox Fruits?

It became a pork chop.

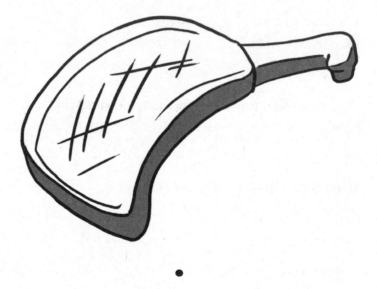

I didn't care about the game until I found my first fruit.
Then my interest spiked!

Robloxer #1: Do you like finding fruit?
Robloxer #2: It's the bomb!

●

When is discovering smoke a good thing?
In Blox Fruits.

●

Robloxer #1: Want to dig for fruit?
Robloxer #2: Sure, I'll give it a spin.

●

Robloxer #1: Why do you like searching for fruit?
Robloxer #2: I don't know, I just dig it.

●

Who's good at finding advanced fruit?
The PAW Patrol.

●

Why did the Robloxer go digging for fruit?
She craved control.

What's another name for finding a gem?

A diamond in the rough!

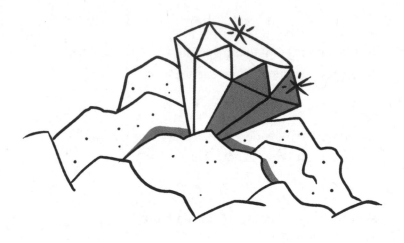

What happened after the Robloxer found rumble and rubber fruits?

He had to clean up the rumble rubber rubble.

Robloxer #1: Did you find any ice fruit?
Robloxer #2: Yes, but it left me cold.

Knock-knock!
Who's there?
Love.
Love who?
Love you!

Want to hear a joke about fruit digging?
Never mind, it's Dark.

What happens if you find a Dark and a Light?
Nothing, they cancel each other out!

Where would you find all the best fruit?
Phoenix!

Remember, fruit doesn't grow on trees.
It grows under them for some reason. This game should be
   call Blox Potatoes.

What kind of cake can you make in Blox Fruits?
Devil's Fruits Cake.

Where can you get a sandwich in Blox Fruits?
The Beli Deli.

What does Hungry Man eat?
Hungry Man dinners!

Knock-knock!
Who's there?
Erin.
Erin who?
I have to run a quick Erin, but I'll be back.

Knock-knock!
Who's there?
Cousin.
Cousin who?
Cousin stead of opening the door, you're making me get cold
out here!

●

What weapon smells the worst?
Musket!

●

What sound does a katana make?
"Meow!"

●

I love this new sword.
It's in flint condition!

●

I was going to buy some weapons in Blox Fruits.
But my finances were all fragmented.

Why are the fruits in Blox Fruit box shaped?

Have you ever tried to stack round objects? It's impossible!

What's the least effective weapon in Blox Fruits?

Arowe.

Knock knock!
Who's there?
Cy.
Cy who?
Cyborg with a Flower Ship for sale.

●

Is Trevor a memorable NPC?
Abs-solutely.

●

That Trevor always tries to make a deal, it's almost like
magic.
He's a real hairy plotter.

●

Knock-knock!
Who's there?
Trevor.
Trevor who?
Trevor you mind about that!

Knock-knock!
Who's there?
Norp.
Norp who?
Norp-body home?

•

I was going to tell this Norp joke
But I'm busy right now.

•

Why are Living Skeletons so chill?
Nothing gets under their skin.

•

When do Living Skeletons work?
During the graveyard shift.
Robloxer #1: I just met a Living Skeleton.
Robloxer #2: Bone-us!

•

Is Blox Fruits hard to find among the many Roblox games?
No, it's just a few blocks away.

I threw my gravity fruit up in the air and didn't know where it went.

And then it hit me.

You know you play a lot of Blox Fruits if . . .

■ When your parents tell you to have some fruit, you ask if this counts.

■ You don't wake up in the morning, you spawn . . . and if you don't get out of bed for 20 minutes, you despawn.

■ You wonder why they can't make medicine out of elemental fruits.

■ It occurred to you that how eating an elemental fruit brings immunity to physical attacks is pretty much just, "An apple a day keeps the doctor away."

■ All the trees in your yard have holes dug under them.

■ You call it the "Blox Fruit Dealer," not the supermarket.

Chapter 6
SOUND THE SIRENS!

Why? Because there's been an escape . . . of laughter at these fun and silly jokes all about the exciting, action-packed Roblox game called Jailbreak.

Knock-knock!
Who's there?
Robin.
Robin who?
Robin banks!

Knock-knock!
Who's there?
Rob.
Rob who?
Let's rob a casino!

Knock-knock!

Who's there?

Heist.

Heist who?

Heist, how are ya?

What's shinier than a
stolen diamond?

Two stolen diamonds.

How do you escape the jail in Jailbreak?
Hit the escape button!

●

How can you tell that a scientist would like Jailbreak?
All the cells.

●

How does one become a criminal?
Well, it's a complicated series of events.
Or one just chooses "criminal" at the selection menu in
    Jailbreak.

●

You really can't loan me your handcuffs?
Sorry, my hands are tied.

●

Why is the taser the best item in Jail Break?
It's stunning!

Knock-knock!
Who's there?
Cuffs.
Cuffs who?
Bless you!

●

What's a good name for a cop in Jailbreak?
Spike!

●

How can you tell a kid likes to play as a cop in Jailbreak?
His hair is spiked.

●

In Jailbreak, I never use the pistol, only the stun gun.
It's just a tase I'm going through.

●

Can you use a sports car to escape?
Not if they're Audi them.

Roblox Player #1: Why do you like Jailbreak?
Roblox Player #2: It's so arresting!

•

Is there phone service in Jailbreak?
Well, there are lots of bars.

•

Do phones work in Jailbreak?
Yes, cell phones!

•

I got some great tools in Jailbreak.
I'm really gunning for victory!

•

Roblox Player #1: Is playing Jailbreak fun?
Roblox Player #2: It's worth a shot!

•

"I just threw a grenade!" the escaped criminal boomed.

What kind of phones do cops use?

Shell phones.

What's a good name for a Jailbreak shotgun?
Mi-Shell.

Knock-knock!
Who's there?
Minnie.
Minnie who?
Minnie-Shield!

Knock-knock!
Who's there?
Shield.
Shield who?
Shield do for our team when we break out!

He said he robbed the donut shop in Jailbreak.
But there were holes in the story.

Stealing a donut was easy.
A hole in one!

Roblox Player #1: Did you read my note on how to rob the donut shop?

Roblox Player #2: I glazed over it.

●

Roblox Player #1: I robbed the donut shop for you.

Roblox Player #2: How sweet!

●

Why is the donut shop a great place to rob?
It's got a lot of dough!

●

I robbed the donut store too early.
It was a half-baked plan.

●

Where's a great place to steal beans in Jailbreak?
The gas station!

Can a horse play Jailbreak?

Yep, they choose to be clops.

Knock-knock!
Who's there?
Gas.
Gas who?
It's me!

Knock-knock!
Who's there?
Camaro.
Camaro who?
Camaro here, I want to talk to you.

●

What does a bird drive in Jailbreak?
Jeep!

●

I was going to steal a bigger vehicle after the escape.
But I wasn't properly trained.

●

Knock-knock!
Who's there?
Pickup.
Pickup who?
Pickup your mess!

Knock-knock!
Who's there?
See.
See who?
See to crouch, F to punch, let's play!

•

Knock-knock!
Who's there?
Right.
Right who?
Right shield will protect you, officer!

•

What does Jailbreak have in common with Adopt Me?
So many shells.

•

Knock-knock!
Who's there?
SWAT.
SWAT who?
SWAT's new with you?

Knock-knock!
Who's there?
Sewer.
Sewer who?
I sewer you're home.

I don't like taking the sewer escape route.
It stinks!

What doesn't have a nose but smells?
The sewers.

What's the most common metal in the jewelry store?
Steal!

Knock-knock!
Who's there?
Jail.
Jail who?
Jail-o in there!

Why were the criminal's eyes glazed over?

He'd just robbed the donut shop.

Why did the thief rob the money train?

It was something he red.

Roblox Player #1: Have you punched many electrical boxes?
Roblox Player #2: A fuse.

•

What happened to the thief who fell into the lake?
He wound up on the moist wanted list.

•

What kind of capes do the criminals wear?
An S cape.

•

Why did the guy robbing the station get caught so quickly?
A cop was on petrol.

•

Was the criminal so excited to rob the gas station?
Sure, he was pumped up!

•

What's a prisoner's favorite song?
"Don't Fence Me In."

Knock-knock!
Who's there?
Pickup.
Pickup who?
Pickup the knob and open it!

●

Why did the robber leave the diamonds alone?
They'd been under a lot of pressure.

●

Why did the thief run for the baseball field?
He heard there was a huge diamond there.

●

Why did the thief head for the rabbit hutch?
He heard there were a lot of carrots there.

●

Roblox Player #1: Why'd he rob the jewelry store?
Roblox Player #2: He just took a shine to it.

What's a criminal's favorite sport?

Fencing.

How is a jewelry store like a jail?
One is full of prisms and the other is a prison.

•

Roblox Player #1: You want to borrow a rocket launcher?
Roblox Player #2: Sure, I'll give it a shot!

•

A better name for a mini-weapon in Jailbreak:
An assault trifle.

•

Found some bombs in my game of Jailbreak today.
It was a blast!

•

What kind of music plays in Jailbreak?
Rocket roll.

•

You know you play a lot of Jailbreak if . . .
■   You look for a secret wall behind the cafeteria.

- While running in class, you feel like holding down the shift key.

- You think being on the "most wanted" list is a good thing.

- You call the honor roll the "most wanted" listed.

Chapter 7
BRAAAAAAAIN WAVE!

The bad news: There's been a zombie attack! The good news: Zombie Attack is a fast-paced game on Roblox. The great news: Here are a bunch of jokes about Zombie Attack and its mindless, lurching, flesh-hungry residents.

How is Zombie Attack like an old friend?

There's lots of waving.

How is Zombie Attack like the ocean?

Everything comes in waves.

Why is Mega Tank so easy to beat?

He's just so green.

What does a Tank Zombie say when he's attacking?

"Look ma, no hands!"

Why did King Slime go to the dentist?
To get a new crown.

●

Why did King Slime hit the beach?
To catch some rays.

●

What sticks out the most about King Slime?
The tongue.

●

Why did Dark Ghost have a hard time walking?
Its bloody soles.

●

I don't get why everyone is afraid of Dark Soul.
I just don't see it.

●

What's another name for King Slime?
A moss boss!

What's a zombie's favorite food?

Pizza, because it's round.

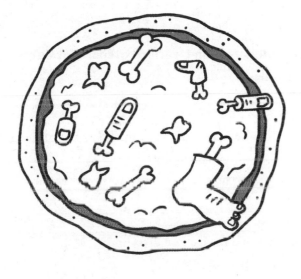

Why do zombies sing "Row Row Row Your Boat?"
They like doing anything in a round.

If that zombie had half a brain . . .
Well, it wouldn't hunt you so thoroughly.

●

That Dark Ghost sent out an earthquake!
It was so shocking!

●

How does Demon Overlord prepare for fights?
He wings it!

●

Those things Demon Overlord shoots out of the ground
   didn't come naturally.
It was something to a-spire to.

●

Better name for Demon Overlord:
A purple people eater.

●

Is the Alien Leader tough?
Well, that's kind of a gray area.

There is no character more popular than the Explosive Zombie.

It really blew up!

Does the Alien Leader at least have fun?

He seems to be having a ball!

Why did the zombie wave finally stop?
Because the overlords were dead tired.

●

The Zombie Attack game is so relentless.
It just goes spawn and on and on and on.

●

Why did the Alien Leader forget to send enemies?
He just spaced out.

●

Did the Alien Leader mean to send so many minions?
Nope, he didn't planet.

●

They should make a movie about the Alien Leader.
He's got star power!

●

Why is easy mode so easy?
Because it isn't hard mode!

Why is hard mode so hard?
Because it isn't easy mode!

Did you hear about the creator of Zombie Attack?
He made a killing!

Knock-knock!!
Boo.
Boo who?
Ah, Dark Ghost!

Knock-knock!!
Who's there?
Easily distracted Zombie.
Easily distracted Zomb—
Hey, look, another player!

Knock-knock!
Who's there?
Interrupting Zombie.
Interrupting Zombie wh--
Yaaaaaaaaaah!

•

What group of villains stings the most?
Zom-bees.

•

What sounds small but could inflict major damage?
A tack.

•

A riddle:
I am alive, but I am dead.
How can this be?
What boss I be?
A zombie.

•

How are the zombies such efficient hunters?
Dead-ication!

Where in Zombie Attack should you
avoid if you don't want to run into zombies?

Dead ends.

What did the zombie say to the Robloxer?

"Nice to eat you!"

Why don't zombies smell?
Because they're dead and their noses don't work!

•

What do you call a zombie with no eyes?
A zombe.

•

You're surrounded by 500 zombies. Who dies first?
Your player, because you can't kill all those zombies.

•

What's black and white and dead all over?
A zombie in a suit.

•

What do zombies and these Zombie Attack jokes have in common?
They're brainless!

•

Did you hear about the big zombie party?
It was pretty dead.

136

Did you know it's actually quite easy to kill zombies in Zombie Attack?

It's a real no-brainer.

•

What should you do if you're surrounded by zombies and get scared?

Remember that you're just playing Roblox, and that this is not real life.

•

Why did the Lava Zombie attack?

It's just its way of saying, "I lava you."

•

Where do Lava Zombies go to the bathroom?

The lava-tory.

•

Lava Zombie is a boss.
Because he likes to fire people!

When do the zombies show up
in Zombie Attack?

Around ate o'clock.

What does a Lava Zombie snack on?

Fire crackers.

Roblox Player #1: Is a Lava Zombie a fireman?
Roblox Player #2: No, he makes fire, man.

●

Why did the Lava Zombie attack?
He was all fired up!

●

How does King Slime's story begin?
Once upon a slime . . .

●

Why does King Slime fly?
Because Slime flies when you're having fun.

●

How does King Slime move here and there?
With his slime machine!

●

Where can you can find tips on how to beat King Slime?
Goo-gle.

What do you call half of King Slime?
King Slim.

What do you call King Slime's destruction?
Slime crime.

What do you call a tiny Demon Overlord?
A little devil.

What else do you call a tiny Demon Overlord?
A Demon Underlord.

What do Demon Overlords wear on their days off?
Demon Overalls.

What did the Lava Zombie's spouse say?
"You light up my life!"

What does the Dark Ghost snack on?

Ghostess cupcakes.

Who is the nerdiest boss in Zombie Attack?
Dork Ghost.

Where does the Mega Tank deposit its Robux?
At the Mega Bank.

•

What Roblox games do Dark Ghosts like to play?
Orbs-tical courses.

•

What finger is an Alien Leader's favorite?
Its pinkie!

•

How does an Alien Leader make money?
He sells its plasma.

•

What's the most nerve-wracking mission styles in Zombie Attack?
Worriers.

•

There are actually two kinds of Cobra weapons
Hers and hisssss.

How do Zombie Attack winners like their fried chicken?
With extra skins!

•

Did you hear about the awkward Zombie Attack player?
She was uncomfortable in her skin.

•

Roblox Player #1: I just got a bunch of new skins.
Roblox Player #2: That's crate!

•

Good news! I finally beat all the bosses and got some skins.
Hey, better crate than never.

•

I don't know what I did to upset that Explosive Zombie.
He just blew up at me!

•

What boss is like a balloon?
The Explosive Zombie, they'll just blow up.

What kind of sea creatures
would you find in Zombie Attack?

Rays!

A sign you play too much Zombie Attack: Whenever
you head to the lobby of a building, you get ready to
respawn.

Knock-knock!!
Who's there?
Mikey.
Mikey who?
Mikey came from killing a boss!

●

Food for thought: If everyone in Zombie Attack dies, the
game ends . . . but then everyone is *already* dead in
Zombie Attack.

Chapter 8
SEAWORTHY SILLINESS

Avast, me hearty shipwrights! This be the chapter of jests about life at sea, or at least the life at sea inside of ye Roblox game, where ye Build a Boat for Treasure. Argh!

What kind of building material can you wear on your head?
A turbine!

•

When is the best time to get boat parts?
When they're on sail.

•

Why do theater kids love Build a Boat for Treasure?
There are so many stages.

•

Someday, Build a Boat for Treasure boats will have paddles. Oar not.

Remember, Build a Boat for Treasure players: There is no
"I" in team . . .
But there are three in "shipbuilding."

●

Which team always recycles its old blocks?
The Green Team.

●

Which team has the most books on board?
The Red Team!

●

Which team is the friendliest team?
"Yellow!"

●

Which team is the saddest?
The Blue Team.

●

Which team accidentally surrenders the most?
The White Team, whenever they wave their flag.

How does the Green Team stay alert?

They drink green tea!

Knock-knock!
Who's there?
Alma.
Alma who?
Alma treasure awaits at the end!

Roblox Player #1: Did you know that the last level is full of concrete, bricks, and diamonds?

Roblox Player #2: Sure, it's the hardest!

●

Knock-knock!

Who's there?

Arthur.

Arthur who?

Arthur any cookies left to build with?

●

I just got a bunch of popcorn and cannons fired at me.

What a circus!

●

Knock-knock!

Who's there?

Candy.

Candy who?

Candy put this cool block on our boat?

What building block is half brick but contains no bricks?
Fabric.

●

I wasn't going to build with magnets.
But something drew me to them.

●

Roblox Player #1: How big is a wheel?
Roblox Player #2: Well, it's wheel big!

●

I wound up playing Build a Lunch for Pleasure.
It all started when I combined sand with a wedge.

●

Roblox Player: Doctor, doctor, you've got to help me.
     There's a back cookie growing out of my spine!
Doctor: Let's build on that.

●

I got so thirsty building my boat.
I used up a boxing glove just to get some punch.

Knock-knock!
Who's there?
Hugh.
Hugh who?
Huge wheel!

●

"Get to the back of the boat," the Build a Boat for Treasure
    player said sternly.

●

"I'm just establishing the load-bearing parts of my ship!" the
    Build a Boat for Treasure player beamed.

●

"I've got to fix the boat motor," the Build a Boat for Treasure
    player said mechanically.

●

"I have exactly enough windows on this boat," said the Build
    a Boat for Treasure player painfully.

"I wouldn't work glass blocks with my hands," said the Build a Boat for Treasure player painstakingly.

●

"This water is rough," said the Build a Boat for Treasure player rapidly.

●

"Look at my shiny new ship!" said the Build a Boat for Treasure player, waxing enthusiastic.

●

"Stay out of my treasure!" the Build a Boat for Treasure player claimed.

●

"This chest is empty!" the Build a Boat for Treasure player hollered.

●

"I'm taking this boat back to the dock!" the Build a Boat for Treasure player reported.

I put a camera on my boat.
It made quite the picture.

Knock-knock
Who's there?
Boat.
Boat who?
Boat time you got out here and helped me build a boat for
    treasure!

How do you stop a boat in Build a Boat for Treasure?
Sing "whoa whoa whoa, the boat . . . "

Knock-knock!
Who's there?
Rhoda.
Rhoda who?
Rhoda boat in search of treasure today!

Would you like some of these extra blocks for your boat?
Planks!
Here you go.

•

What does a treasure boat drink?
Coala.

•

You *can* put bread on your ship.
But only if you're a loafer.

•

It's only recently that players started putting bread on their
    boats.
It's on the rise!

•

You need a cute way to get on the boat.
So pick something a-door-able!

•

What's the most musical building block?
A harpoon.

I lifted the treasure too quickly.

Now I've got chest pains.

I couldn't acquire an egg cannon block.
So I just placed some outward facing chickens up there on
the deck.

Knock-knock!

Who's there?

Barry.

Barry who?

Barry the treasure again before anyone can steal it!

●

There's just something great about building with rods.

It really sticks with you, and for very long.

●

Knock-knock!

Who's there?

Truss.

Truss who?

Truss me, I'm good at shipbuilding.

●

Where do you go if you put a wooden seat on top of a throne?

You "go" right there!

You can't just go to a store and find a quest.
Well, you can if it's Target.

●

Knock-knock!
Who's there?
Fabbi.
Fabbi who?
Fabbi birthday!

●

The Secret Place is the best game ever.
Not to put it up on a pedestal.

●

I love using the balloon block.
It really floats my boat!

●

I once used all of the same materials.
And then there came a big witch.

What do treasure seekers do on the weekend?
They build a boat for pleasure.

What happens if you discover a ton of treasure?
You gild that boat with treasure, and it will be a pleasure!

What happened to the boat covered in ice blocks?
The sailors had chilled a boat for treasure.

Did you hear about the hungry sailors who were adventurous eaters?
They grilled their boat for pleasure!

What caused the boat to stop moving?
The suspension!

Why are the prisons in Build a Boat for Treasure so nice?
They're lined with gold bars.

What did the flag on the
boat say to the ocean?

Nothing, they just waved
at each other.

What boat part should you use during foggy conditions?
I-Beams!

Roblox Player #1: What does that cow do on your boat?
Roblox Player #2: Steer!

•

Knock-knock!
Who's there?
Fireworks.
Fireworks who?
Fireworks if you want to burn our boat for some reason!

•

What food is served on the boats in Build a Boat for Treasure?
Seas-ur salad.
What else is served?
Fish and ships.

•

Knock-knock!
Who's there?
Chest.
Chest who?
Chest got back from a quest!

Knock-knock!
Who's there?
Heart.
Heart who?
Heart you glad to see me?

●

Roblox Player #1: What happened to all those marble rods
　　you were using?
Roblox Player #2: They rolled away!

●

What's in the mystery box?
It's a mystery!

●

I put a bunch of obsidian on my ship.
And then everything went black.

What's the worst thing about a Delay Block?

. . .

. . .

. . .

I'm sorry, what was the question?

●

You know you play a lot of Build a Boat for Treasure if . . .

You cool down your drinks with "ice blocks" not ice cubes.

- When you go for a run, you break it up into 11 stages.

- You don't consider bowling a sport so much as you do a stage.

- To you it's not a soccer game, it's a quest!

- In school you hear about Helen of Troy, "the face that launched 1,000 ships," and you wonder why they didn't just use a launch button.

Fill in the Blank

Find the name of the Build a Boat for Treasure item that completes the couplet about the game's building materials. (Answers follow.)

1. I can be light and airy or heavy as lead
I'm cooked in an oven and turn into . . .

2. You'll find in the sea, and also on land
I'll remind you of beaches, because I am . . .

3. I could be more specific, I'm essentially a box

You use me for everything, because I'm basically . . .

4.   Stick to me and I'll stick to you
I'm like liquid tape, except I'm . . .

5.   I hang proudly, unless I sag
Don't forget to salute me, because I'm the . . .

6.   Even though you're a mere mortal
You can travel to another land with the use of a . . .

7.   You run the risk of finishing last
If you forget to build a sailboat that doesn't have a . . .

8.   Watch out for me if about to schlep
I'm the first part of a journey, just one humble . . .

9.   Don't get too close, as I'm bound to scorch
I'm really quite useful, not quite a lamp, but a . . .

10. Program me to do anything, like make your boat swerv-o
I'm a vital component that's known as a . . .

Answers:

1. BREAD
2. SAND
3. BLOCKS
4. GLUE
5. FLAG
6. PORTAL
7. MAST
8. STEP
9. TORCH
10. SERVO

Rhyme Time

Can you figure out what material from Build a Boat for Treasure we're talking about when we give you rhyming clues? (Answers follow.)

1. Pig Witch
2. Doubloon Lock
3. Moo Leg
4. Trusted Knock
5. Field Venerator

6. Veering Meal
7. Should Nod
8. Nice Rock
9. Pet Urban
10. Knife Reserver
11. Clocked More
12. Pirate Feet
13. Rocker Mall
14. Snack Feel
15. Flouncy Sock
16. Counted Fjord
17. Goat Rotor
18. Too-sick coat
19. Mourner ledge
20. Fame toward

Answers:

1. BIG SWITCH
2. BALLOON BLOCK
3. BLUE EGG
4. RUSTED BLOCK
5. SHIELD GENERATOR

6. STEERING WHEEL
7. WOOD ROD
8. ICE BLOCK
9. JET TURBINE
10. LIFE PRESERVER
11. LOCKED DOOR
12. PILOT SEAT
13. SOCCER BALL
14. BACK WHEEL
15. BOUNCY BLOCK
16. MOUNTED SWORD
17. BOAT MOTOR
18. MUSIC NOTE
19. CORNER WEDGE
20. GAMEBOARD

How can you make a game of
Build a Boat for Treasure last longer?

Use a life preserver!

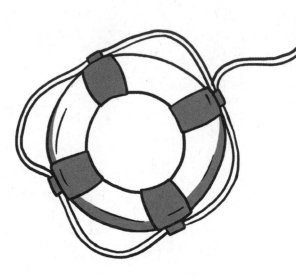

Chapter 9
RANDOM ROBLOX RANDOMNESS

Just some kooky and wacky bits about some of our favorite other Roblox games, adventures, quests, and simulations.

Why did The Overseer decorate his uniform that way?
Because the eyes have it!

•

I just came across a total copy of Medieval Warfare.
Talk about a Reforgery!

•

Bed Wars is a great game.
Don't sleep on it!

•

Where would you find this book in Roblox?
In Bookhaven!

What kind of fish can you find in an obby?

Walleyes.

Knock-knock!

Who's there?

Me!

Me who?

Adopt me!

Knock-knock!
Who's there?
Boat.
Boat who?
Build a boat for treasure!

Knock-knock!
Who's there?
Piggy.
Aaaah, get out of here!

Did you hear about the Roblox player who got fired from his job at a pizza place?
He forgot to go to work because he spent too much time playing Work at a Pizza Place.

I lost hard at Bee Swarm Simulator.
It just really stings!

Knock-knock!
Who's there?
Brick.
Brick who?
Brick battle!

Is Roblox fun?
Sure, it's a walk in the parkour!

What store do Robloxers love to go to?
Obby lobby.

Where do Robloxers park their cars?
In a parkour lot.

When is the worst time to play an obby?
In the fall!

What Roblox game would
a pirate like?

Arrrr-senal.

I love finding a nice striped wall in an obby.
It's such a great hop-portunity.

Why do bunnies love obby games?
All of the wall hops.

•

That was one tough obby.
It really packed a wall-hop!

•

Roblox is a healthy way to spend the time.
It's good to have an obby.

•

Roblox Player #1: Do you like Kitty?
Roblox Player #2: It's purrrfect!

•

Roblox Player #1: Have you played the new Clone Tycoon?
Roblox Player #2: I have, but it seems familiar.

Knock-knock!
Who's there?
The floor.
The floor who?
The floor is lava!
Aaaaaah!

Knock-knock!
Who's there?
Granny.
Granny who?
Granny who, do you want to come over and play Roblox?

Knock-knock!
Who's there?
Roy.
Roy who?
Royale High.
Roy, I'm Al, hi!

What kind of sunglasses
do Robloxers wear?

Wraparounds.

Is there a more robust world than Epic Mini Games?
To find one you've be Hard-Pressed.

Are there a lot of choices in Epic Mini Games?
It's an Avalanche!

Knock-knock!
Who's there?
Laser.
Laser who?
Laser on, when you're free, let's play Laser Tag!

What Roblox game do sheep play?
Fleece the Facility.

What Roblox game has the biggest sandwiches?
Supper Hero Tycoon.

Did you hear about the veggies that fled the salad bar?
It's all in the new Roblox game Kalebreak.

Why did the Bed Wars player
throw wood planks?

They wanted to sleep like a log.

**Why did the zombie get booed at the Roblox Talent
   Show?**

His jokes were rotten.

Roblox Player #1: Are you wining at Epic Minigames?
Roblox Player #2: I'm just trying to stay Above Water.

•

Roblox Player #1: Have you played the dodgeball mini
game?
Roblox Player #2: I've been avoiding it!

•

Piggy had a sore throat.
She wound up disgruntled.

•

We found Piggy in the kitchen.
She was bacon.

•

Piggy was trying to hide and got stuck in a tree.
Now she's a pork-u-pine.

•

Roblox Player #1: Hey, Phantom Forces was here just a
minute ago. Where did it go?
Roblox Player #2: It disappeared!

What game would vampires like?

Blood Escape!

What's a great Roblox game for babies?

Lumber Tyke-oon!

Knock-knock!
Who's there?
Brick.
Brick who?
Brick or treat!

Chapter 10
RIDDLING ROBLOX AND QUESTION QUESTS

Enjoy these light-hearted puzzles, wacky word games, and playful pieces that cover many corners of the Roblox universe.

Roblox Anagrams

Can you figure out the name of the Roblox game when we give you two phrases made up of the same letters? (Answers follow.)

1.

Pat Demo

Mad Poet

2.

Maze at Cob Kit

Cat to Make Biz

3.

Tony Machete Pork
Monkey Peach Trot

4.

Baja liker
Ark jab lie

5.

Drew abs
Rad wcbs

6.

My ice pet
Yep me tic

7.

Who foretell
Flower hotel

8.

Aw, locket paparazzi
Zip pock wart azalea

●

9.

Cowbell outbox germ
Tug lox meow cobbler

●

10.

Oh, bravo Ken!
Book her van

●

11.

Cad craw money
Ma, candy cower

●

12.

Ruse quarters
Re-use squatter

13.

Oh yeah girl!

High lo year

14.

Save tier

I ate revs

15.

Neo rift artifacts

Aircraft inset font

Answers:

1. Adopt Me
2. Zombie Attack
3. Theme Park Tycoon
4. Jailbreak
5. BedWars
6. Meep City
7. Tower of H***

8. Work at a Pizza Place
9. Welcome to Bloxburg
10. Brookhaven
11. Crown Academy
12. Treasure Quest
13. Royale High
14. Vesteria
15. Fantastic Frontier

It's Opposite Day in Roblox

Can you figure out the names of the Roblox games when given only the opposites of the words in their titles? (Answers follow.)

1. Hoggy
2. Unadorned Low
3. Freedom Fix
4. Sleep at a Dessert Nowhere
5. Head into the Empty Lot
6. Happy Small Town
7. Artificial Happy Ending Death
8. Southern Seas

9. Little Misery Direct Path
10. Destroy a Plain for Debt
11. Straightforward Weaknesses
12. Living Embrace
13. Baby
14. Ocean Awful-Place
15. Peninsulas
16. Doggy
17. Connecting Area
18. Landpeaces
19. Don't Be Stretched Out by a Slow-Moving Floor

Answers:

1. Piggy
2. Royale High
3. Jailbreak
4. Work at a Pizza Place
5. Flee the Facility
6. Mad City
7. Natural Disaster Survival
8. Northern Lands

9. Mega Fun Obby

10. Build a Boat for Treasure

11. Phantom Forces

12. Zombie Attack

13. Granny

14. Brookhaven

15. Islands

16. Kitty

17. Breaking Point

18. Skywars

19. Be Crushed by a Speeding Wall

True or False?

Which of these statements about the history of Roblox are true, and which are false? (Answers follow.)

1. "Roblox" got its name from a combination of the first and last name of its creator, Robert Loxington.

●

2. The idea for Roblox came about when an inventor gave a robot a bunch of Legos to play with.

3. Before the internet, people used to play Roblox with pads and pens, writing down what their character did in various games, and then they'd mail the papers to each other.

4. The very first Roblox game was a simulation game called Waiting in Line at the Bank With Mom Simulator.

5. The one millionth game uploaded to Roblox was called Sit on the Couch and Watch Your Friend Play Roblox.

6. There's a cheat code that brings free Robux and game elements that randomly works. All you have to do is type "PLEASE."

7. The game was supposed to be called "Roblods" but when the creator registered the game, he made a typo.

8. In France, Roblox is called Le Reauxbloc.

•

9. The identity of the creator of MeepCity is secret, but it's widely believed to be movie star Vin Diesel.

•

10. Every Taylor Swift album contains an Adopt Me! reference.

•

11. There were literally bugs in the first version of Roblox. People who sent away for the game cartridge sent them back because they arrived full of ants.

•

12. The Builder Brothers from Work at a Pizza Place are based on real restaurant-running brothers Ron and Don Guilder, who run a sub sandwich place in Michigan.

Answers:

They're all false. We made them all up!

Roblox for All!

If you have a thread and needle instead of a computer you
 could play . . . Sew-blox.

If you'd rather play a round of trivia, that's just Know-blox.

If you were really short, you'd play Low-blox.

If you played on TV, that would be Show-blox.

If you played on a raft in a river, that's Go with the Flow-blox.

If you've got a really old computer, you're probably playing
 Slow-blox.

If your skills get better, it's because you're playing Grow-
 blox.

In the winter, you play Snow-blox.

If you did this for money, you do Pro-blox.

When the game starts up you should say, "Hello-blox!"

Birds like to play Crow-blox

In France they play Chateau-blox.

With your boyfriend or girlfriend, you might play Beau-blox.

Cowboys play Whoa-blox.

When you've done everything you can in the game, you're
 going to Plateau-blox.

If your car dies and you're killing time playing video games,
 that's Tow-blox.

If it makes you really happy you must be playing Glow-blox.

Paint a picture of your game scenario and you're Vincent Van Gogh–blox.

Play this on a ship, and it's Stow-blox.

To learn about your future, you would play Tarot-blox.

UNOFFICIAL JOKE BOOKS FOR MINECRAFTERS
Available from Sky Pony Press

WRITE YOUR OWN JOKES HERE!

_____

_____

_____

_____

_____

_____

_____

_____

_____

_____

_____

_____

_____

_____

_____

_____

_____

_____